LANDSCAPES AND SEA VIEWS

GUILDHALL ART GALLERY

ACKNOWLEDGEMENTS

This book was written by Vivien Knight, Curator of the Permanent Collection. Information was provided by the staff of the following institutions: Bristol Reference Library; University of Reading, Rural Life Centre; Worcester City Library; Falmouth Art Gallery; Tate Gallery; by the author's colleagues in Guildhall Library and by Dr David Cordingley. Gill Keay, formerly of Guildhall Art Gallery's conservation staff provided the details of the inscription on the painting by John Brett. Naomi Allen was the Gallery's liasion with the designer and producer and with Jeremy Johnson obtained the photographic material for illustrations.

ISBN 1-902795-02-4

Cover: Benjamin Williams Leader *The Churchyard, Bettws-y-Coed* (p. 28)
Title page: Albert Goodwin *The Toiler's Return* (p. 32)
Back cover: Edward William Cooke (detail from) *Dutch Pincks, Scheveningen* (p. 24)
Photographs courtesy of Bridgeman Art Library

Published by Guildhall Art Gallery, 1999
Designed by Mick Keates
Produced by Supreme Publishing Services

LANDSCAPE PAINTING emerged as a distinct genre within British art in the late 17th century. Its roots lay in the topographical townscapes and country house portraits which celebrated prosperity and a settled social order in the wake of the Restoration of the monarchy. Most of these were painted by immigrant artists from the Netherlands like Jan Vosterman (1643-1699) who painted the earliest of Guildhall Art Gallery's landscape paintings, *London from Greenwich Hill*, in 1680. In the following century cultivated taste favoured the idealised classical landscapes of Claude and Gaspar Dughet and their English imitators. Interest in Britain's own wild and mountainous scenery was awoken with the cults of the Sublime and the Picturesque, but it was not until the early years of the 19th century that many painters turned to her peaceful pastoral farmlands.

Influenced by the Dutch 17th century landscapes by artists like Hobbema, Ruisdael and Wynants, in the first third of the 19th century more rural landscape subjects were painted than any other kind of picture. Their popularity reflected growing unease among the urban middle classes about the dehumanising aspects of life in the expanding cities and towns and a nostalgia for the apparently purer and more natural life of the countryside. However, their reassurance of stability and peace was at odds with the turbulent changes in the countryside throughout the century. Enclosure, food riots, unrest over low agricultural pay and the mechanisation that threatened unemployment, railway mania, urban expansion and the drift of labour from the land that became a tide in the agricultural depression of the last quarter of the century – these were issues that few landscape painters embraced in their work. Most of them lived in the city close to their patrons, their dealers and the exhibitions, venturing into the countryside on the annual summer sketching tours which provided them with subjects, and painting their pictures in the studio during the winter from the sketches and on the spot oil studies they had made on their trips. Aiming to please their patrons rather than to record social issues, their selective vision generally passed over the unpleasant aspects of rural life, and ignored the railway lines, factories and urban sprawl that must increasingly have obtruded into the foregrounds of their views. Sir John Gilbert's view of *Worcester* (page 30) is an exception, doubly surprising in the work of an artist better known for his subjects from history and legend.

The technological advances which threatened traditional country life and spelled the end of isolation for many English villages also carried the landscape painter and his patron to fresh fields. With the end of the Napoleonic Wars in 1815 and the development of railways and steamships more people than ever before could venture abroad with relative ease and travel became a fashion that stimulated a demand for foreign views. Responding to a demand for pictorial souvenirs and feeding the interest of those unable to travel, one of the most successful in exploiting the market was David Roberts (pages 22 and 26). Roberts's *forte* was in painting architecture, while his fellow scenery painter Clarkson Stanfield (pages 18 and 23) and Stanfield's younger friend Edward William Cooke (pages 20, 21 and 24) concentrated on British and continental coastal landscape scenery. Virtually neglected in the previous century, coastal and marine subjects had become popular with the Romantic era and were influenced by 17th century Dutch marine painters like Simon de Vliegher and Jan van der Cappelle.

Cooke's careful observation of the details of boats, clouds and rock formations testify to a general climate of empiricism and objectivity and an interest in material fact. Instead of the suggestive painterliness of Constable's period, painting in the 1830s and 1840s was characterised by clear outlines, bright colours and meticulously rendered detail – elements which also enabled pictures to contend with the brighter gas lighting introduced in London townhouses from the 1840s. The formation of the Pre-Raphaelite Brotherhood in 1848 heralded the climax of this development. The landscape backgrounds of Millais' *The Woodman's Daughter* painted in 1851 (illustrated in *Children in Paintings*) and of the Pre-Raphaelite follower William Shakespeare Burton's *The Wounded Cavalier* of 1856 (illustrated in *Victorian Pictures*) were painted 'on the spot' and exemplify the painstaking attention to sharply lit microscopic detail advocated by the influential critic John Ruskin.

The influence of Ruskin and the Pre-Raphaelites was widepread throughout the 1850s but their intensity of focus was unsustainable. In the 1860s most artists abandoned painting finished pictures out of doors, feeling that nature was too fugitive to be captured on the spot. John Brett (*Echoes of a Far-Off Storm*, page 36) – whose earlier work had been guided by Ruskin, with whom he shared an interest in the new natural sciences of geology and meteorology – was one of those who reverted to painting their canvases in the studio from outdoor studies, replacing the uniform bright light of the Pre-Raphaelites with a broader tonal handling suited to a wider variety of atmospheric effects.

Tonal handling and absence of detail were characteristic of the French landscape paintings shown in London from the 1870s. The Barbizon school was popular but the Impressionists – exhibited in London from 1872 – had little success with either collectors or artists. It was the Salon *plein air* painters – of whom Jules Bastien Lepage was the most influential – who excited young artists dissatisfied with the teaching in the Royal Academy Schools. Bastien's photographic realism, his broad, unmodulated brushstrokes acknowledging the actual flatness of the canvas, and the concept of painting figures outdoors rather than in the studio drew British students like Walter Osborne (page 40), Henry Scott Tuke (page 42) and Henry Herbert La Thangue (page 46) to study in Paris or Antwerp. Later they painted in rural communities in Brittany where primitive customs, unspoilt landscape and picturesque traditional costumes could still be found. When they returned to England they established similar colonies of artists in the Cornish fishing villages of Newlyn and St Ives, in Walberswick in Suffolk and elsewhere. In 1886 many were founder members of the New English Art Club, whose tenets included a commitment to painting out of doors. Their influence even more pervasive than that of the Pre-Raphaelites, the so-called 'British impressionists' set the tone for landscape painting into the 20th century.

The development of 'British impressionism' coincided with the agricultural depression of the last quarter of the 19th century. A series of severe winters and cold wet summers coupled with the competition of cheap foreign grain and meat imports (made possible by the development of railroads and steamships) spelled ruin for many farmers and landowners. Many sold out to their tenants and saw their grand houses converted into schools and nursing homes. Farmworkers fled the land to seek work as grooms or carters or – like the young man in Gore's 'Listed (page 38) – to join the army, leaving behind only the old and unskilled. England's urban population had exceeded the rural one for the first time in 1851: fifty years later it was three times as large and agriculture represented only a fraction of the nation's economy. La Thangue's wistful and elegiac *Mowing Bracken* (1903) seems obliquely to acknowledge that the old order of country life had already passed away.

PATRICK NASMYTH 1787-1831
The Meeting of the Avon and the Severn 1826

oil on canvas
Bequeathed by Charles Gassiot, 1902

Nasmyth exhibited views taken around Bristol, Clifton, Clevedon and Bradford on Avon at the Royal Academy and the British Institution between 1827 and 1831. This view has previously been thought to depict the meeting of the Rivers Avon and Severn below Bristol at Avonmouth. However, the 1830 Ordnance Survey map of the area shows no village at the rivermouth and a low-lying landscape, unlike the sloping wooded common shown here. Nasmyth may have taken the view further round the coast at Portishead Point although Portishead at the time was still not as large a settlement as the one depicted here.

Nasmyth said, 'what is the use of going to Italy for subjects, when we can get them outside our own doors? anything will make a picture, if it is properly treated', His brother, the eminent engineer James Nasmyth, recorded in his autobiography (1883) that as a boy Patrick 'acquired great skill in sketching trees, clouds, plants and foregrounds. [...] The wild plants which he introduced into the foregrounds of his pictures were his favourite objects of study. But of all portions of landscape nature, the Sky was the one that most delighted him. He studied the form and character of clouds – the resting cloud, the driving cloud, and the rain cloud – and the sky portions of his paintings were thus rendered so beautifully attractive. [...] In his landscapes he introduced picturesque farm-houses and cottages, with their rural surroundings [...] He made excursions to various parts of England, where he found subjects congenial to his ideas of rural beauty. [...] These consisted of rural 'bits' of the most picturesque but homely description – decayed pollard trees and old moss-grown orchards, combined with cottages and farm-houses in the most paintable state of decay, with tangled hedges and neglected fences, overrun with vegetation clinging to them with all "the careless grace of nature". [...] When sketching he was in his glory, and he returned to his easel loaded with sketchbook treasures, which when painted form the gems of many a collection. [...] On my brother's first visit to London, accompanied by my father [the Scottish landscape painter Alexander Nasmyth], he visited many collections where the old Dutch masters were to be seen, and he doubtless derived much advantage from his careful studies, more particularly from the works of Hobbema, Ruysdael, and Wynants. These came home to him as representations of Nature as she is.'

PATRICK NASMYTH 1787-1831
Watermill at Carshalton 1830

oil on canvas
Bequeathed by Charles Gassiot, 1902

There were many mills on the banks of the River Wandle at Carshalton in Surrey, associated with paper-making, calico printing and flour grinding. The mill shown here stood on the estate surrounding The Culvers, a mansion at Carshalton bought in 1866 together with 77 acres of surrounding land by Charles Gassiot's brother John Peter Gassiot. Charles may have bought the picture in 1871, when a painting entitled 'Carshalton Mill, Surrey' appeared in the same Christies sale that included a painting by Collins which he bought shortly afterwards. Charles and his brother had fallen out irrevocably by 1886, when John Peter wrote him out of his will. John Peter Gassiot died in 1899, and in 1902 the Culvers estate was sold.

JOHN CONSTABLE 1776-1837
Salisbury Cathedral from the Meadows 1829-31

oil on canvas
Bequeathed by Charles Gassiot, 1902

This picture is the full sized sketch for the more 'finished' version of the composition (private collection) which Constable exhibited at the Royal Academy in 1831. It was his practice to paint large preparatory oils such as this as part of the process of developing a large composition from the drawings and small oil studies which he made on the spot. Although Constable himself did not consider them as pictures to be shown to the outside world, their free and expressive handling greatly appeals to modern eyes.

Constable based the picture's composition on drawings of the view – looking from the north-west across the river Avon to Salisbury Cathedral from the wooden Long Bridge (seen in the lower right corner of the painting) – made while he was staying in Salisbury with his friend Archdeacon Fisher in July 1829. In August Fisher wrote to Constable telling him that his easel had arrived and urging him to return, noting: 'It will be an amazing advantage to go every day and look afresh at your material drawn from nature herself.'

The picture's intense colour and stormy atmosphere may have had a personal connotation for Constable. While Archdeacon Fisher's description of the composition as 'the Church under a cloud' was probably humorous (although perhaps reflecting his own concern for the Church of England in this year of Roman Catholic emancipation, or his anticipated drop in income from farm rents because of the poor harvest), the picture's troubled mood may be related to Constable's own emotional state in the wake of his wife's death the previous year. (A different mood is captured in the 'finished' version, where the storm is clearing and the landscape is fresh and green, and Fisher's house Leadenhall – not easy to distinguish in the Guildhall picture – is picked out at the end of a rainbow, a symbol of renewal and hope which also recalls Rubens, whose '*Landscape with a Rainbow*' in the Wallace Collection Constable knew. When the picture was exhibited at the Royal Academy in 1831 Constable chose to accompany it in the catalogue with a passage from James Thompson's *Summer* (1727) which underlines its personal content. The passage describes the sky clearing after a summer storm which has struck Amelia dead in front of her lover Celadon, and the widowed Constable must have identified with this sorrowful episode as well as with the sentiment of acceptance and peace which succeeds it.)

When the sketch came to the Gallery through the Gassiot Bequest it bore the title *Fording the River, Showery Weather*, and in place of the cathedral's spire was a square church

tower. X-ray and expert examination in 1951 showed that this tower and other parts had been painted over original paint and varnish, and the overpaint was removed to reveal the picture in its present form. It has been suggested that the overpainting may have been done by a dealer to make the picture more saleable as a unique composition; but as the picture was apparently bought at an early date by its first owner, James Price of Barcombe, Devon, and acquired by Charles Gassiot through Agnews' in 1895 shortly after Price's death, the schedule of events cannot be confirmed.

Thomas Christopher Hofland 1777-1843
Boys Fishing at Highgate Ponds c.1832

oil on canvas
Purchased, 1996

Hofland was a keen fisherman and had perhaps himself fished this reservoir, one of the Highgate Ponds formed by damming Highgate Brook on the east side of Parliament Hill to supply water to North London. Rising above the trees is the spire of St Michael's Church, Highgate, built in 1832.

In their book *A Century of British Painters* (second edition 1890) Richard and Samuel Redgrave noted that 'Hofland's landscapes were not of the imitative or realistic school. They are mostly studied compositions; he aimed, at least, at treating nature under a poetical aspect and divested of commonplace. But the tone he adopted throughout gave great monotony to his works; while his handling wanted variety, his surface lacked texture, and the softness with which the parts too often melted into one another, added to the prevailing

want of colour, gave a feeling of insipidity to his pictures. As a painter he never rose to the first rank, since propriety rather than genius was his great characteristic.' However this unaffected picture – painted much in the manner of Constable – demonstrates another side to Hofland's character, the same side that is expressed in the charming vignette illustrations and enthusiastic text of the book he published in 1839, *The British Angler's Manual*.

PETER DE WINT 1784-1849
Near Lowther Castle
watercolour
Presented by Miss T A C Durning Lawrence, 1946

De Wint earned his living largely as an itinerant drawing master with pupils throughout the country whom he visited on his extensive annual sketching tours. Said to be received by his patrons as an equal and a valued friend, the artist often stayed with the Earl of Lonsdale at Lowther Castle near Penrith in Cumbria where he painted many views in the neighbourhood. In this view, Lowther Castle is seen in the middle distance with the river Lowther at the right.

WILLIAM COLLINS 1788-1847
Shrimp Boys at Cromer 1815

oil on canvas
Bequeathed by Charles Gassiot, 1902

William Collins was a painter of children in coastal and rural landscapes, his style and subject matter varying little throughout his career. His pictures were praised for their lack of artifice and their truth to nature – Constable himself said 'Collins's skies and shores are true, and his horizons always pretty.' However, like most of his contemporaries Collins painted his pictures in the studio rather than directly from nature, from the studies he made on his sketching tours.

In autumn 1815 Collins and his friend the artist James Stark visited the small fishing village of Cromer in Norfolk. During his two month stay Collins made numerous sketches of the beach and cliffs (but not, recorded Stark, of any figures). These furnished material for his pictures for many years afterwards, although *Shrimp Boys* was one of the first which he painted from his studies there.

In *A Century of British Painters* the Redgraves explained: 'his practice was to make drawings of all the parts and details which he intended to use in his work, to study the effects of air and light on the spot, and then to paint his picture in his studio from these materials. He sketched in, first the general composition of his picture, the disposition of the parts, the rack of clouds, the figures he intended to form part of the composition; often arranging and rearranging, until he was satisfied with this stage of his labours. From this he proceeded to the dead colouring. He began, as is usual, with the sky, which he endeavoured to finish at once, and, failing to do so, would hang a wet sheet before it during the night, to keep it wet for the next day, and this part of the work he finished with the sweetener [a badger hair brush, used dry for softening and blending]. He then painted from the horizon forward, finishing the various distances towards the foreground. To secure the true light and shade of his figures, he adopted at times the method of his friend Wilkie, grouping clay figures or dressed dolls in a box lighted for that purpose.'

William Collins 1788-1847
Barmouth Sands (Welsh Peasants Crossing the Sands to Market) 1835

oil on canvas
Bequeathed by Charles Gassiot, 1902

Collins and his family visited Wales in summer 1834. At Barmouth, a small fishing village on the north shore of the Mawddach estuary, he was, according to his son Wilkie Collins in his memoir of the artist, 'once more by the seaside, with coast scenery of the most novel and picturesque order to employ his attention. [...] In the natural characteristics of this place, and in its motley population, composed partly of fishing and partly of market people, he found the material for one of his next year's pictures, called 'Welsh Peasants, Crossing the Sands to Market'. In spite of the obstacles of frequent wet weather, he succeeded in making as many studies at Barmouth before he quitted it as he desired. [...] The great beauty and originality of the lines of the composition in this picture [...] struck everyone who saw it.'

Collins depicts women, girls and a boy on their way to market with produce that includes ducks – carried in a large basket on one woman's head (protected by a pad or 'durch') – and live chickens. Throughout Wales red was the most popular colour for locally made woollen clothes, although colours and patterns varied from place to place: the women here wear red flannel or woollen skirts with black jackets, one with a red shawl beneath her tall beaver hat. The black hats banded with ribbon first became popular at the beginning of the 19th century, their height and shape varying with the area, but – as seen here – many women also continued to wear the straw hat.

Perhaps Collins' Welsh Peasants modelled for him in their best clothes, because he shows them wearing leather shoes, expensive items which were not common among the poorer classes who would often go to market in bare feet.

CLARKSON STANFIELD 1793-1867
In the Gulf of Venice 1848

oil on canvas
Bequeathed by Charles Gassiot, 1902

In August 1838 Stanfield left England for a long tour of Italy. He travelled to Venice from Milan, and then went to Rome and Naples, the Gulf of Salerno and Ischia. Returning to Naples he sketched the eruption of Vesuvius before beginning the journey home via Tuscany, Florence and the Rhone valley, returning to England in March 1839. Although Stanfield never visited Italy again he exhibited subjects drawn from the studies he had made there until 1865: this picture is dated 1848.

Stanfield brings to this picture compositional devices which suggest his experience as a scenery designer, and when the *Art Journal* reproduced an engraving of the painting in 1854, the accompanying account noted his skill in employing these as well as hinting at the uncertain identification of the view:

'That portion of the Adriatic coast which constitutes the Gulf of Venice presents features of scenery not unlike those found in other parts of Italy, lying on the sea; but it is also distinguished by peculiarities that unmistakeably show its contiguity to Venice, such as edifices rising immediately out of the water. We have an example of this in Mr Stanfield's picture, where the group of buildings, like those of Venice, are evidently erected on piles, and are connected with the mainland by a small bridge. On the elevated bank to the right of this are two other groups of buildings, separated from each other, having the appearance of ancient Italian castles, and a range of hills, some of which are of considerable height, form by their varied undulations and broken outlines, a picturesque background to the picture.

'No artist understands better than Mr Stanfield the value of judicious accessorial introductions, either as points of light or shadow, or as boats to give distance: the boat to the right answers all these purposes; the bottle and the small bits of stone reflected in the shadows, not only relieve the rather monotonous tone of the quiet waters, but materially assist in throwing back the rest of the composition into their [sic] proper places.'

The little town depicted here remains unidentified, and perhaps the mountainous scenery locates it towards the south of the Gulf of Venice. Two words written in pencil on one of the stretcher members may identify the scene: they are now virtually illegible although it is possible to read the second as 'Ancona'. In 1848 Stanfield exhibited at the

Royal Academy a painting of Ancona which had been commissioned by a collector named Samuel Wheeler and was bought after his death in 1871 by Agnew's. In 1872 Agnew's sold Charles Gassiot a painting of the same title, and it would be tempting to identify this picture with that (now untraced) painting - if it were not for the fact that the description of the picture exhibited at the RA was completely different from the Guildhall painting.

EDWARD WILLIAM COOKE 1811-1880
Tower of Erchia [sic]: *Gulf of Salerno* 1849
oil on canvas
Bequeathed by Charles Gassiot, 1902

Cooke travelled to Italy in 1845, remaining there a little over a year. Like Stanfield he was attracted to the coastal landscape of the Gulf of Salerno. With the isle of Capri shown in the distance, this coastal view near Erchie, a hamlet between Amalfi and Ravello, demonstrates Cooke's interest in rock formations as much as in the colourful local details of boats and fishermen.

EDWARD WILLIAM COOKE 1811-1880
Triassic Cliffs, Blue Anchor 1866

oil on canvas
Presented by John Byram, 1963

The picture's traditional title is inaccurate, for the cliffs at the small Somerset seaside resort of Blue Anchor are not Triassic but Liassic – a term denoting the Lower Jurassic period and a kind of limestone which is usually banded with shale or clay. At Blue Anchor, the contorted strata of the cliffs dip down to the sea where they overlie a harder sandstone.

While few fossils are found in Triassic limestone, Liassic limestone in England is noted particularly for its fossils of ammonites and reptiles. Cooke recorded collecting fossils at Blue Anchor and spending rainy evenings sorting them.

DAVID ROBERTS 1796-1864
Edinburgh from the Calton Hill 1863
oil on canvas
Bequeathed by Charles Gassiot, 1902

Commissioned by the entrepreneurial art dealer Ernest Gambart and repeating a composition which Roberts had painted five years earlier for another patron, this picture was painted in London, from where Roberts wrote to a Scottish friend on November 19 1862: 'I am at present on two smaller works one of Holyrood from the Calton Hill and the companion from the same hill looking west ... so that if "my heart [is not] in the highlands a' chasing the Deer" it is in the town of my boyhood – which is better!' The picture exemplifies Roberts' manner of painting, using large masses of cool tones enlivened by figures and accessories that provide spots of bright local colour. The circular building is the monument to Dugald Stewart, designed by Playfair in 1832 and the Gothic structure is the monument to Sir Walter Scott erected in 1844.

CLARKSON STANFIELD
1793-1867
Old Holland 1858
oil on canvas
Bequeathed by Charles
Gassiot, 1902

The son of an actor-writer, after playing child parts in the theatre and an apprenticeship to an heraldic painter, Stanfield went to sea in 1808. During his eventful maritime career he painted the scenery for on-board amateur theatricals and voyaged as far as China. Back on shore and in London, in 1816 he obtained work as a scenery painter in Stepney, the prelude to a highly successful career at the Royal Coburg Theatre, Astley's Amphitheatre and the Theatre Royal, Drury Lane. Stanfield painted *Old Holland* in the same year that he contributed his final work for the theatre and it surely reflects both his own experiences as a seaman and the dramatic influence of the stage. He advised an artist friend that scenery painting was good training for art provided it was combined with the study of nature (but warned another friend that it had a coarsening influence that was hard to overcome in easel painting). Stanfield may have based the painting on drawings made in 1843 during the last of his three visits to Holland.

Ruskin praised the accuracy of Stanfield's meteorological observation, finding him 'next to Turner [....] incomparably the noblest master of cloud-form of all our artists; in fact he is the only one among them who can really draw a cloud. [...] I cannot point to any central clouds of the moderns, except those of Turner and Stanfield, as really showing much knowledge of, or feeling for, nature. [...] One work of Stanfield alone presents us with as much concentrated knowledge of sea and sky as, diluted, would have lasted any one of the old masters his life' (*Modern Painters*, 2nd ed. 1888).

EDWARD WILLIAM COOKE 1811-1880
Dutch Pincks, Scheveningen 1860

oil on canvas
Bequeathed by Charles Gassiot, 1902

Shown here is a type of boat known as a pinck which was mainly used in drift net fishing off Scheveningen, a fishing village near The Hague with a long sandy beach of which Cooke was especially fond. During his many visits there and elsewhere on the Dutch coast he filled sketchbooks with studies of boats, weather conditions and coastal activities which he used in his paintings. These accurately observed local details together with Cooke's careful paint handling and smooth surfaces made his pictures very popular. *Dutch Pincks...* clearly illustrates his attention to detail, refined handling and silky surface, although close examination of the horizon shows that he moved some of the buildings, their earlier positions showing in blue outline as *pentimenti* beneath the now transparent surface paint.

The name 'Van Kook' on the stern of the nearer boat is a playful Dutch version of the artist's own name which he often gave to his Scheveningen fishing boats, perhaps in recognition of the inspiration he had received from 17th century Dutch painters of the sea like Jan van de Cappelle. (It was also the name given to the new lifeboat for which Cooke presented the Royal National Lifeboat Institution with a cheque for £200 in December 1863.)

DAVID ROBERTS 1796-1864
The Forum, Rome 1859
oil on panel
Bequeathed by Charles Gassiot, 1902

The market place of earliest Rome, the Forum Romanum became the political centre of the city and of the Roman Empire. With the Empire's decline and fall and the victory of Christianity its temples, basilicas and other monuments were abandoned, fell into ruins and became overgrown. For centuries the forgotten Forum was known simply as *Campo Vaccino*, the 'cow field'.

Although the area around the Column of Phocas was substantially cleared during the Napoleonic occupation of Rome and a scheme to excavate the Forum down to its original level more than twelve feet below was begun in the 1830s, the first systematic excavations were undertaken between 1848 and 1853. Their discoveries – poignant reminders of the lost civilisation and its great empire – captured the imagination of tourists and artists alike.

It was shortly after this phase of excavation and clearing that Roberts made his second trip to Italy, arriving in Rome in October 1853 and remaining there until early February 1854. This picture is one of seven views of different parts of the Forum which he painted on his return to England from the studies he made there. It was painted together with a companion for William Wethered, a London tailor who also ran a picture dealing business.

In the foreground is the well known picturesque landmark of the three surviving columns of the Temple of Castor (known then as the Temple of Jupiter Stator). To the left is the church of Sta Maria Liberatrice (demolished 1900-1901). To the right in the middle distance are the columns of the Temple of Saturn and the Temple of Vespasian. Behind

is the (mediaeval and later) Palace of the Senator, above which rises Martino Longhi's 16th century campanile. On the far right is the lone Column of Phocas.

When Roberts recorded the composition of this picture in a pen and ink sketch in his diary he gave it a more humpy foreground than appears in the painting. In fact the Forum was comparatively overgrown until the 1860s or even later and was not fully excavated until the present century.

Benjamin Williams Leader 1831-1923
The Churchyard, Bettws-y-Coed 1863

oil on canvas
Bequeathed by Charles Gassiot, 1902

Many Victorian artists were drawn to North Wales in search of picturesque views. One of its most famous beauty spots was Bettws-y-Coed, 'the chapel in the wood', an overgrown village at the junction of the rivers Llugwy and Conwy in Gwynnedd. It had been 'discovered' by David Cox, and by mid-century it was one of the most painted places in Britain. Leader painted many views of the graveyard of the 14th century church which gave Bettws its name. In this picture its melancholy beauty prompts thoughts of mortality which are underlined by the sundial at the left and the musing children upon the tomb and the warm late afternoon colouring which gives way to a twilit gloom in the valley.

The picture's vivid colouring reflects the obvious influence of Pre-Raphaelite landscape painters although it lacks their unselective attention to detail. Deploring the poor quality of that year's Royal Academy exhibition, in 1863 the *Art Journal* noted: 'Our English school [...] suffered some few years since, at the hands of the so-called Pre-Raphaelites, a revolution. But the wild oats then sowed brought forth a sorry harvest; and some zealots who thought to gather wheat found but tares. [...] Still in all frankness let it be conceded that [...] when the extravagance is spent, a certain residue of good lives on. [...] The new school of detail, free in great measure from the eccentricity and extravagance of earlier years, shows this season some satisfactory results of close out-door study. [...] 'A Welsh Churchyard' by B W Leader shows some capital studies of yew trees watching, as it were, like mourners among the tombs.' In 1871 the same magazine noted that the compositional formula of setting 'dark masses, trees and other objects [...] against an evening sky, with the sunlight still glowing on the distant hills' was a favourite of the artist's, and picked out this picture as an example.

The picture was bought from the 1863 Royal Academy exhibition by the then Chancellor of the Exchequer, W E Gladstone – a sale which reflects the artist's swift and increasing success. In 1875 Gladstone sold the picture at Christies, where it was bought by the dealers Thomas Agnew's – who in turn sold it immediately to Charles Gassiot.

Sir John Gilbert 1817-1897
Worcester 1868
watercolour over pencil
Bequeathed by George Gilbert, 1903

Built at an ancient fording place on the River Severn, Worcester had been a prosperous inland port even before the opening of the Birmingham and Worcester canal in 1815. Despite improvements made to navigation in the 1840s, the opening of the Oxford, Worcester and Woverhampton railway in 1850 offered an alternative form of cheap and rapid freight transport, ushering in the end of the canal era here as elsewhere. Worcester soon became a railway centre with huge shunting yards, sheds and engine works.

Gilbert depicts the view from the north-east and hints at the conflict between tradition and new technology, contrasting the railway of the modern world with the silhouetted cathedral of the ancient city and a watching pair of rustics beneath a prophetic, brooding sky. The factory-like building may be the Vulcan Iron Works established in 1857, which manufactured signals and other railway apparatus and machinery.

JOHN LINNELL 1792-1882
The Timber Waggon 1872

oil on canvas
Bequeathed by Charles Gassiot, 1902

Linnell and his family lived in Porchester Terrace, Bayswater – a formerly peaceful suburb which became increasingly built up in the 1840s. Deciding to move to the country, in May 1849 Linnell took the train to Edenbridge in search of a suitable spot within easy reach of London. During a delay at Redhill Junction he walked up Redstone Hill, where in Redstone Wood he chanced upon an eleven acre estate for sale. Within two months he had bought the land, and by 1852 had moved into the new house he had built on it. Over the next few years he bought more land until he owned 80 acres in all, much of it woodland.

Linnell was the most prolific and successful landscape painter in Britain, his poetic idylls ignoring the steady erosion of the countryside and its old ways of life. Yet the technology that brought the tranquillity of the countryside within reach of Londoners like Linnell also spelled the end of its isolation. The London to Brighton line had reached

Redhill in 1841 and over the next few years branch lines were built to Ashford and through Reigate to Reading. Between 1851 and 1861 the population doubled to 10,000, the incomers – like Linnell himself – building themselves large new villas and mansions in the surounding woodland. Perhaps scenes like the one he depicts in *The Timber Waggon* struck a painful chord in the artist who claimed he rarely felled a tree on his own land.

ALBERT GOODWIN 1845-1932
The Toilers' Return 1877
oil on canvas
Presented by Charles T Harris, 1908

Goodwin is better known as a watercolourist whose technique was influenced by Turner's: this is a rare example of his oil painting, a medium he was advised against by his friend and patron John Ruskin who wrote to him in 1876: 'I have always felt deep regret at your taking to oil and to large canvases. The virtue of oil, as I understand it, is perfect delineation of solid form in deep local colour. It seems to me not only adverse to, but even to negative, partially, beautiful landscape effects.'

This picture looks down from the cliff top at Lynton, North Devon over the harbour at the small fishing village of Lynmouth. The tower is 'Reginald's Tower', which was destroyed in the Lynmouth flood disaster of 1952 and has since been replaced with a replica, while the long thatched building may be the Rising Sun public house. Long poles or withies mark the deep channel along which the returning fishing boats will enter harbour. Goodwin had moved to Ilfracombe in Devon in 1876. He must often have seen fishermen's wives looking out for their menfolk, and in an understated narrative aspect to this glorious coastal landscape a young mother gazes out for the distant sail that marks her husband's safe return in advance of the dark clouds gathering on the horizon.

JAMES WEBB 1825-1895
Mont St Michel 1868

oil on canvas
Presented by James Northcott, 1929

Webb shared with Clarkson Stanfield a preference for breezy and dramatic coastal views, and he painted this picturesque subject on at least two other occasions (Tate Gallery and Mappin Gallery, Sheffield). Mont St Michel – a granite island off the Normandy coast, dominated by a mediaeval Benedictine abbey – is seen here from the north or off-shore side, at the centre of a dramatic composition which reflects Turner's influence.

Webb also appears to have maintained a shadowy profession as an 'able and prolific forger' of 'Turners' and 'Constables' from at least as early as 1869. Comparing 'the incomparable genius of Constable' with 'the lamentable deficiencies of Webb when imitating him', in 1906 a writer in *The Burlington Magazine* described how 'It was always on the aesthetic side that Webb failed. When painting a landscape in his own manner he is by no means a painter to be despised: he has knowledge of cloud-form and of atmosphere; he can build his subject with that degree of truth which impresses us at once with the feeling that here was a man who could translate some of the mystic beauties of nature and bring them before us in comprehensible form. But his manner changes when he is working in imitation of Constable or Turner. He is endeavouring all the time to catch the trick of the brush, the breadth and sureness of handling, and consequently he is easily detected by the abject failure of the clouds and sky.'

John Brett 1830-1902
Echoes of a Far-Off Storm 1890
oil on canvas
Presented by Sir Thomas Devitt, 1918

Brett's early work was influenced by Ruskin and the example of the Pre-Raphaelites and focussed closely on botanical and geological detail. Later he abandoned the unselective all-over detail of Pre-Raphaelitism and replaced their prismatic colours with more muted tones suited to a wider range of atmospheric effects.

From the 1860s onwards Brett concentrated on coastal views around Britain. Characterised by their restricted colour range, careful draughtsmanship and the complete absence of any human element, they reflect the artist's scientific interests in their observation of weather effects and rock formations. Spending every summer with his family on some remote part of the British coast, Brett was especially fond of the rocky coastlines of Devon, Cornwall and Pembrokeshire. During these summer visits he painted numerous sketches and small oil studies, whose dimensions of 7 x 14 inches were in proportion to those of his large paintings – usually 42 x 84 inches (the size of the Guildhall's picture). Brett prided himself on working directly without retouching: in 1883 Beatrix Potter recorded: 'Mr Brett does not paint his large pictures from nature, but from small sketches and memory. He seems to have an extraordinary memory and to paint very fast, finishing a large picture is a few days. He is an enthusiastic photographer and has a big yacht'; and she went on to note 'Mr Millais says all the artists use photographs now.'

Brett spent the summer of 1889 with his family at Padstow where, wrote the artist Arthur Hughes, he made 'beautiful studies about the coast among the ripples and rocks. He does one small one complete at a sitting on fine and good days – beautiful skies and

lovely seas, and foreground of the pretty mermaid tresses colouring the pools or what not.'
He returned home to Putney on October 1, and *Echoes of a Far-Off Storm* is inscribed along
one of its tacking edges 'Begun Xmas Day 1889'. Exhibited at the Royal Academy in 1890,
it probably depicts a beach along the coastline between Padstow and Newquay, one of
which, *Harlyn Bay*, was the subject of another of Brett's RA exhibits in that year.

WILLIAM HENRY GORE c.1860-1931

'Listed 1885

oil on canvas
Bequeathed by Charles Gassiot, 1902

Gore lived in Newbury, Berkshire, and set this picture in the low-lying meadows of the Kennet valley nearby. It shows a young man who wears recruiting ribbons in his cap to signify that he has enlisted as a soldier bidding farewell to his sweetheart, her sorrow echoed by the chilly early morning landscape.

Gore painted this picture during the severe agricultural depression of the last quarter of the 19th century, when many farmworkers from the arable lands of the south and east abandoned the countryside to look for work in the towns or to join the army. Perhaps the young man in this picture has enlisted in the Royal Berkshire Regiment, which in 1885 was active in Egypt and the Sudan following the uprising against the British and the death of General Gordon.

WALTER FREDERICK OSBORNE 1859-1903
An October Morning 1885
oil on canvas
Presented by the Artists' Cricket Club as a Memorial
to the artist, 1904

Osborne shared with other young British artists who
studied on the continent in the 1870s and 1880s a commitment to painting rustic subjects in the open air rather
than in the studio. After studying in Antwerp in 1881-2
and painting in the artists' colonies of Pont Aven and
Quimperle, in 1884 he returned to England and painted
in Lincoln, Southwold and Walberswick in Suffolk. There
he met Philip Wilson Steer who, influenced by Monet
and the Impressionists, was using broken brushwork and
prismatic colours. Steer's example may have influenced
the way Osborne painted the pebbles in this picture the
following year.

While at first glance the picture seems as casual and
off-centred as a snapshot, Osborne carefully leads the eye
into the composition by a succession of objects along a
zig-zag route. While he uses this device to create pictorial
depth, his handling of the pebbles emphasises at the same
time the actual flatness of the picture surface.

With the title *October by the Sea*, the picture was
Osborne's first exhibit in 1887 with the New English Art
Club. It was presented to Guildhall Art Gallery by the
Artists' Cricket Club as a memorial of their regard for
him. Among the Club's members were Henry Scott Tuke,
H H La Thangue and Arnesby Brown – *plein air* painters
with whom Osborne – at his death a successful Dublin
portraitist and society figure – had been associated as a
young man.

Henry Scott Tuke 1858-1929
Ruby, Gold and Malachite 1902

oil on canvas
Purchased from the artist, 1902

Tuke studied at the Slade School and then in Belgium and France where he was an admirer of the French painter of *plein air* peasant subjects Jules Bastien Lepage. In 1884 he visited the artists' colony of Newlyn but settled the following year in a cottage overlooking Falmouth Bay. Tuke had spent a happy childhood at Falmouth, where he had learnt to swim from its secluded beaches. Now these remote spots allowed him to work entirely out of doors on canvases in which he explored the effects of sunlight on skin and on shallow, translucent water.

Ruby, Gold and Malachite – the title referring to the colours of the sweater, the sunlit bodies and the green sea – was painted in the summer of 1901 on Newporth Beach, which was virtually inaccessible except by boat. In his Register Tuke recorded that the models for the picture were Georgie Fouracre (his landlady's son), Charlie Mitchell (who looked after his boats) and Bertie White and Harry Cleave (two local boys who frequently modelled for him at this time). In a letter to Guildhall Art Gallery dated 20 March 1912, Tuke wrote 'Of the models, the one standing half in the boat is now an Engineer high up in the Union Castle Line. The one in a red jacket has been many times round the world in the boats of the Clan Line, and the one standing up with the paddle is a bold artillery man who has served several years in Malta and other Mediterranean stations – all of which goes to show that posing in or about the water is not a cause of early death as some of my friends are fond of pointing out, but is a good training and gives much time for useful meditation'.

Guildhall Art Gallery bought the picture in May 1902, after its Director Alfred Temple had reminded his Committee that they had spent nothing from the Purchase of Exhibits fund for the three years it had been in existence. A deputation from the Committee went to the Royal Academy to consider twenty pictures, but in the event only two were purchased – after their prices had been negotiated downwards – *Ruby, Gold and Malachite* and Arnesby Brown's *The River Bank* (page 44).

Tuke recorded that 'Hugh Lane was untiring in persuading Mr Temple to recommend his committee to buy it', while Lane (who later became Director of the National Gallery of Ireland but died on the *Lusitania* when she was torpedoed in 1915) wrote to the artist: 'I wish you could feel one tenth the happiness that I am possessed of at the result of worrying poor old Temple. You will probably only think of the small monetary gain (or loss!) of

the picture, but I am convinced (and T agrees with me) that now a really fine example of your art is in so conspicuous a collection all the Provincial Galleries will follow the Guildhall's lead and want a specimen of your work. Temple called twice to see me about it yesterday and seems as pleased as I am.' On August 1 1902 Tuke noted in his diary: 'Two days ago I got my cheque from the Guildhall, rather a remarkable document, half a side of blue foolscap signed by the Committee, about 7 of them. They are going to get the picture from the RA a day earlier, so as to have it when Lord Kitchener is received on the Wednesday evening.'

SIR JOHN ALFRED ARNESBY BROWN

1866-1955
The River Bank 1902

oil on canvas
Purchased, 1902

Brown was exclusively a painter of the English landscape, often with cattle in the foreground. Born in Nottingham, he was a pupil of the landscape painter Andrew MacCallum before joining Sir Hubert von Herkomer's school at Bushey in 1889 for three years. Soon afterwards he moved to Haddiscoe, near Norwich, dividing his time (until 1931) between Norfolk and the colony of *plein air* painters at St Ives in Cornwall where he found the longer hours of daylight an advantage in winter.

Painted in Norfolk, *The River Bank* exemplifies Brown's early manner as a painter of high summer's brilliant greens and thundery skies. In an article in the *Magazine of Art* written in the year this picture was painted, the critic A L Baldry wrote: 'His work is characteristically British, and has remained both in manner and method unaffected to any perceptible extent by foreign traditions. [...] At the age of thirty five he is accepted as one of the chiefs of the romanticist school. [...] He has a temperament that helps him to appreciate the dreamy and poetic suggestions of nature in her gentler moods. [...] He wisely does not attempt the task of painting his large pictures in the open air [but] he prepares himself by prolonged and careful study of his subjects and by making a large number of sketches to aid his memory.'

Noting that his cattle were 'painted with something of the breeder's appreciation of their weight and bulk,' his obituarist in *The Times* described him in terms that themselves suggested the placidity of beasts: 'He was a big slow-moving man, suggesting the country squire, exceedingly quiet in his manner and scant of speech, though he was a good companion and universally liked.'

HENRY HERBERT LA THANGUE 1859-1929
Mowing Bracken 1903

oil on canvas
Purchased, 1903

La Thangue studied at the Royal Academy Schools and for three years in Paris under the Salon painter Gérome. After painting in the artists' colonies in Brittany in 1881 and 1882 and later in the Rhone valley, La Thangue returned to London in 1884 and after occupying a studio in Chelsea for a year worked at Walsham, on the Norfolk Broads and at Rye before moving in 1891 to a farmhouse near Bosham, Sussex. Like Bastien Lepage, he believed that an artist had to live among the scenery and people he depicted, and as a country dweller he must often have witnessed scenes such as that depicted in *Mowing Bracken*.

While scythe handles were usually made from ash and steamed into shape, in this picture La Thangue's young labourer has fashioned a primitive handle from a suitably shaped piece of timber he has found growing naturally. Attached to it is a bow, made from a hazel rod, which helped to lay down the mown crop ready for collection. This scythe may have been kept solely for cutting bracken. Dried, bracken furnished winter bedding for farm animals and was also used for thatching. In the background of the picture a load of cut bracken is being carted away. There is a feeling of separateness about the departing figure of the girl leading the horse which, read together with the boy's closed expression as he concentrates on his work, perhaps indicates a narrative element to the scene in addition to its apparently objective observation.

In 1896 the landscape painter George Thompson wrote in the magazine *The Studio*: 'Mr La Thangue has presented us in his art with striking renderings of many phases of a rustic life which has still many picturesque elements. For the steam plough and the threshing machine have not driven manual labour out of the country. The ploughman has by no means worked his last furrow in sleepy Sussex, and the travelling harvester with scythe on shoulder [...] is even now taking form upon the painter's latest canvas.' Nevertheless, by the time *Mowing Bracken* was painted, many farmworkers had deserted the countryside in search of better pay and conditions, and their old skills and trades were already in decline. Its elegiac mood underscored by its autumnal colouring, *Mowing Bracken* seems to be a lament for the changing life of the countryside.

INDEX OF ARTISTS

INDEX OF TITLES